DEAREST DEBBIE

Honey, if God had told me that day when we asked for you nine years ago—after having seen your Korean picture at age three—if God had said then, "You may have her for nine years, but then she must come home," I would still have wanted you, and still have brought you here. You brought something we can't forget—a quality of spirit—to this house.

Dale Evans Rogers

DEAREST DEBBIE

DALE EVANS ROGERS

PYRAMID BOOKS *NEW YORK*

DEAREST DEBBIE

A PYRAMID BOOK

Published by arrangement with the Fleming H. Revell Company

Revell edition published March, 1965

Pyramid edition published June, 1966
Second printing July, 1966

Copyright, ©, 1965 by Fleming H. Revell Company

Library of Congress Catalog Card Number: 65-14798

All Rights Reserved

Printed in the United States of America

PYRAMID BOOKS are published by Pyramid Publications, Inc.,
444 Madison Avenue, New York, New York 10022, U.S.A.

DEAREST DEBBIE

Nimble brown legs, flashing in the sun.
Two-wheel bike coasting downhill:
"Look, no hands!"
Hearty laugh, quick smile: "Aw, quit teasing!"
Frown of concentration as unaccustomed fingers
Try to curl the dark hair:
"These things go the way they want to!"
An impish smile in a tilted-back chair.
Cross-legged on a bed, carefully applying nail
    polish
As a curly-headed doll watches from the fireplace.
First transistor radio: "Hey, listen; it's the Beatles!"
Starched dress and white Bible at Sunday school.
Joyfully singing in the Children's Choir.
Seated backwards in a kitchen chair: "Let me
    help!"
Wet bathing suit and water-sleeked hair: "Come
    on and swim!"
Maternally feeding baby a bottle, cuddled in the
    rocking chair.
Dark head bent over the game table: "I won! I
    won!"
Thrilled with flowers, scents and sights of Hono-
    lulu.
Generous heart: "You can have it."
Squeals and laughter at the Fair.
Six sticks of bubble gum at once!
Upside down on the couch, long legs dangling
    over the back.

Giggles at bed time.
Quick sympathy from understanding dark eyes.
No longer little girl. Not quite young lady.
Warm brown arms around my neck: "I love you,
        too."

Kathryn Johnston, Director,
Children's Choir,
The Chapel in the Canyon

Preface

This is the story of our Debbie, a precious gem from Korea, a wonderful little Korean-Puerto Rican girl who found her way into the family of Roy Rogers.

Pen and paper cannot possibly hold or adequately describe the manifold blessings that Debbie Lee brought to us during her nine-year visit. Now that she is gone, my earnest prayer is that other hearts will be touched and extended towards those like her in all parts of the world. My heart aches for all orphans—orphans of war, divorce, death, indifference, or whatever the cause. I wish so much that every child in every orphanage in Korea, Japan, Germany, Africa, Greece, England, America—wherever they are in the world—could be adopted into families able and ready to give them tender, loving care.

World Vision, Inc., is an organization dedicated to the business of bringing blessings like Debbie to such homes, by bringing children from their orphanages into adoptive families, and by collecting funds from other concerned people to feed, house, and instruct in the love and admonition of the Lord other children who must remain in orphanages overseas. One of the heartbreaking problems of the children who are not adopted lies in the grim fact that once they are too old for further orphanage care they are thrust out into a society strongly race-conscious—where they find themselves unacceptable! The majority of these children are of mixed racial backgrounds, like our Debbie; most of them are sentenced to life in a hostile and unsympathetic society, without our help.

We *are* our brothers' keepers! We all have a responsibility for these orphaned ones. Jesus said, "Feed My lambs!" I believe that He meant us to feed them the food of love as well as literal bread; and that He meant that we were to feed them on His Word—the Holy Bible.

There are racial conflicts and conflagrations all over the world. Why? I believe they are due to a lack of love in the world—love of God and for each other. We have nothing whatever to do with the coloring of our skins. This is God's business. He created the world, the plants and animals and people within it, and He saw that it was good—*all* of it! I think God knows what He is doing, and I wonder where we "get off," and who we think *we* are, when we think or boast that we are smarter or better looking or just naturally "superior" to the people of any other race. I'll admit that we Americans are certainly more fortunately situated than many other nations and people, and we are blessed with greater wealth and opportunity—which, again, makes me wonder why we fail to help those who do not enjoy our abundance and advantages in assuming the task of feeding and teaching them to help themselves.

I would not hesitate to suggest to any childless family (indeed, I have suggested it many times) or any would-be adoptive parents that they should welcome a child of another race, or of mixed racial background, into their homes, *if* that family or *if* those parents really love God and children.

Parents are caretakers for God, be they either natural or adoptive parents. It's *love* that counts. Help the orphans any way you can, either by long distance or by giving them a home in your home.

It will bring great joy and blessing. I know—from experience.

Dale Evans Rogers

And we know that all things work together for good to them that love God, to them who are the called according to his purpose.

ROMANS 8:28

Dearest Debbie,

How lovely you must be in your new halo! You always looked so pretty in your simple little white headband.

In July of 1964, you, Dodie, Dusty, Sandy, and I were flying back to Los Angeles from a wonderful ten-day vacation in Honolulu. The stewardess on the plane, rather uncertain because of your size and ladylike manner, didn't quite know whether you would accept the "Junior Wings Pin" they give to all children on those flights. You smiled that sweet, sunny, special Debbie smile and accepted it eagerly, as did your sister Dodie.

Little did any of us know that in one short month you would be gifted with a pair of heavenly wings!

Come to think of it, you were practically flying this whole past year—at home, at school, at church, at play—everywhere. You were so full of energy, your abundant black hair flying along with your quick, coltish brown legs, always wanting to be "in the big middle" of everything. You were only half an inch shorter in height than your mother, and I had just lifted the hems of some of my choice skirts for you. You had grown so much in every way this past year, that on your birthday—that was August 14—I gave you a little money to purchase your own clothes. Dodie and I went along, and we were all quite pleased that you came home with a three-pice outfit and a jumper and a blouse, in an hour and a half. Remarkable!

Daddy had just gone through his highly dangerous neck operation at UCLA Medical Center about ten days before the never-to-be-forgotten day of August 17—and he had been moved from UCLA to a convalescent home where he could get well quicker in a place quieter than a hospital. The boys were busy with some church activities—so on your birthday we decided that you, Dodie, and I would celebrate your birthday together. You wanted a big Italian dinner, and to play miniature golf afterwards. You wanted a German chocolate cake, with candles. The night before, we bought the cake, adorned it with peanut brittle (your favorite candy) and candles, and there was a large tray full of little things dear to an almost-teenager's heart—hair bows, pins, curlers, cologne. You made a wish, and blew out the candles, and we had ice cream with the cake, and a lot of fun watching TV. Then I gave you the extra five dollars for records or anything else you wanted. Remember?

The next afternoon (which was Friday), Dodie and you and I went to see your new nephew, little David Andrew Eaton, sister Marion's new baby boy. Your eyes were wide with astonishment as you looked down at him and said, "Oh, Mama, he's so *tiny!*" How you loved babies! You must be having a wonderful time on the Streets of God, with so many cherubs around—babies whose mothers are still here on earth. You had such a marvelous mother-instinct; you were "a good hand" with infants. It comforts me to know that you are with little Robin—and with little Samuel, who is Judy and Dave Whisenant's little boy and who made a brief one-day visit here. He touched many lives in that one day, just as you have left an indelible impression on so many of us during your twelve-year mission.

Honey, if God had told me that day when we asked for you nine years ago—after having seen your Korean picture at age three—If God had said then, "You may have her for nine years, but then she must come home," I would still have wanted you, and still have brought you here. You brought something we can't forget—a quality of spirit—to this house.

When Dr. Bob Pierce showed us some film from the World Vision orphanages in Korea and told us of the plight of those United Nations children, God crystallized an idea in our minds—that perhaps Dr. Bob could find a little Korean girl about Dodie's age to be her sister. Dodie was three and a half then, and the next youngest in the family was her brother Sandy, who was five years older. We thought that maybe we could help a Korean child, and that a Korean child could help us. I don't know how much we helped you, honey, but I know how much happiness you brought to us and to others.

You were a little "pied piper of Hamelin" on the playground at Chatsworth Park Elementary

School. I used to sit in the car in front of the post office, across the street from the school gate, and watch you; you were always surrounded by friends, or you ran to them in friendly greeting. Since you went away, so many of them have told us how they loved you. I shall always treasure that letter from your school principal who praised you so just before your sixth-grade graduation: "I would like to commend your daughter for the years of excellent service and outstanding citizenship she has given Chatsworth Park School. Each year the staff selects one outstanding child as the recipient of our "Service Above Self" award. Debbie was one of the finalists for this award, and is deserving of this honor. Congratulations on her being one of the most outstanding A-6 students." My eyes were misty when I read that; I was so proud of you! As I write now the tears fall—but they are for me rather than for you, because I miss you so much. You don't need our tears, for you have indeed arrived. Though my flesh grieves, my heart sings for joy that you are with the Lord.

Do you remember the night at the kitchen table when I told you and the boys that Dodie had been accelerated half a grade? The boys, "big-brother-like," were disdainful: "Just wait till she hits junior high; then she'll find out she isn't so smart!" You didn't say anything for a moment, and then you burst into tears because you weren't being accelerated, too. I told you that perhaps next year you would be accelerated, because your grades were so good and you were such a fine student. You wanted so much to go to junior high with Dodie this year—and how *she* looked forward to catching the 7:30 bus with you, and to "showing you around" in the new school. But, Debbie, you have *really* been accelerated, now. You've skipped many, many, hard lessons on this earth. For one thing, darling, you will never have to go through a war of any kind—within yourself, or out in the world. You are spared all the tensions and bigotry and hypocrisy—perhaps an unfortunate marriage or love affair, or a long lingering illness—so many things that so many of us have to go through in this school of time. You will never have to worry about the race problem, for there is no color line in heaven. God tried to do it on our earth. He created a beautiful garden of people—people of all sizes and colors—just perfect. Isn't it too bad that we can't appreciate all His people? That we can't seem to understand that underneath their vari-colored skins all people are alike, with the same capacity for living, loving, and suffering?

You helped God teach us *that*, Debbie!

Can you remember your trip to America on the plane with Dr. Bob and the other children from Korea? I shall never forget the anticipation and excitement of that wonderful day. Daddy, Cheryl,

Linda, Marion, Dodie, and I met the plane. The boys were away at school.

My heart was pounding when the plane landed. Then the door opened and Dr. Bob walked out with a very pretty, solemn, frightened little girl in his arms. You had bangs and a short Dutch bob. As he handed you over to us, I smiled and said, "Hi, Debbie Lee!" You didn't smile back; you clung to us. I had forgotten that you couldn't speak English. We were filming our television series at the time, and we went directly from the airport to the studio. You sat on my lap, and Dodie tried to talk to you and get you to take a little stuffed animal, but you sat very still and watchful, sizing us up—it was *embarrassing*. When we reached the studio the crew made a great fuss over you; everybody stood on his or her head, trying to amuse and relax you. They got nowhere—until the "prop" man gave you and Dodie balloons. Then the sun broke through your serious little face. You laughed, and laughed, and laughed, and from that moment on you were home.

We were a little puzzled when we came to choosing a name for you. Your Korean name was In Ai Lee, so we decided to keep the Lee and give a good Bible first name—Deborah. So you became Deborah Lee Rogers. Right off the bat, we called you "Debbie," because you liked it.

You had been staying in the home of Mr. and Mrs. Raetz, missionaries in Korea, for weeks before you came to us, and they did a wonderful job of teaching you American ways. One day at lunch

I remarked to Daddy that you had the most lady-like manners I had ever seen in a child of three and a half, even though you have come from an entirely different culture than ours. World Vision had given me a pamphlet with several Korean words and short sentences, and I could communicate a little, but not enough, with you. When we finally got home that evening, you walked through our long, rambling ranch house; at the dinner table you were polite and very well behaved, but you said nothing and ate very little until, about halfway through the meal, you looked at me anxiously and spoke to me timidly in Korean. I looked blank, and you went to the older girls and repeated it, with a look of desperation on your face. Finally James (one of our helpers and a Filipino) got what you were saying: "Mrs. Rogers, I think she wants to be excused to the bathroom!"

There weren't too many incidents like that; you caught on very quickly. At play, you tried speaking to Dodie in Korean; she just stared at you and kept saying, "What you say? What you say?" You would look exasperated, shrug it off, and turn back to your toys. It was something, watching you two coming from such different backgrounds and trying to meet on new, common ground.

None of us will ever forget the day you ventured for the first time outside the kitchen door. Bullet came rushing up to you, wagging his tail furiously, begging in his silent dog-language for a pat on the head, and he was as surprised as the rest of us when you let out a howl of terror; it took us quite a while to get you calmed down. Later, it was explained to us that big dogs like Bullet were trained in Korea as police dogs to guard against looting; they were taught to be vicious and to hate everyone but their trainers, and of course you thought poor friendly Bullet was like them! It was weeks, months, before we could convince you that our dogs were friendly dogs.

Just think, Debbie: when God restores perfection on this old earth, the Bible says that "the lion shall lie down with the lamb." Isn't that wonderful? There will be no more hatred or misunderstanding or ugliness on the earth; everything will be beautiful, and *stay* beautiful. There will be no decay. The roses that you loved so much will never fade, their petals will never fall. I remember how I used to scold you for picking roses and other flowers in other people's front yards on your way home from school. I was trying to teach you to respect the property of others, but you would smile that baffling, winning smile of yours and say, "Oh, Mommy, just one doesn't hurt! Besides, it was growing almost out in the road." I think you may have stretched that one a bit, but what could I say when you would run and get a little vase and put the flower in it and set it up over the sink where I could enjoy it while I washed the dishes? You used to pick flowers for your teacher, too; every time someone sent me a bouquet of flowers, you would beg "just a *couple*" to take to school. Do you know, Debbie, since you've been gone, every now and then there seems to be a very strong fragrance of roses all through the house—particularly in your room? I will wake up in the middle of the night and catch that fragrance; I catch it now, as I am sitting in your room writing, at 4 A.M. Of course, at first, I tried to rationalize it, telling myself that probably a heavy dew had fallen on the roses outside and that the wind was carrying it into the room. But it has never happened before, and it happens often now—mostly in the evenings. I am so grateful for it—there is something about a rose—.

You held on to your Korean speech and to your Korean customs for what seemed to be a long, long time. We had quite a time keeping you in bed at night; you would invariably "root for the floor." Our floors in America are not heated (like the floors in Korea where people sleep) and you frequently woke up with a cold during the first six months. I tried a guard-rail on your bed, but you climbed over it or through it with the greatest of ease, and slept on the bare hard boards. You must have felt insecure on a mattress that "gave" with your weight. We struggled with that "floor sleeping" almost as much as we struggled with the language.

You used to cry when I had to leave for work, and it would upset me because I knew you couldn't speak English. One morning you took my hand and led me out into the driveway, waving your arms wildly and pouring out an excited stream of Korean words. Helplessly, I said, "Honey, Mommy can't understand you"—whereupon you stopped in your tracks, put your hands

21

on your hips, and looked me up and down in desperation (and, I think, disgust) at my ignorance, shrugged, and turned away from me back into the house. That was the last time you ever spoke a word of Korean. You started saying our words—phrases and sentences immediately; within six weeks you were speaking English as well as Dodie spoke it. It was an amazing performance. I wonder how many adults could do that!

But there was one sweet phrase we *all* kept and used, out of your Korean; it was *pö-pö-käsh-uwä* and it meant "Give me a kiss."

Dodie had a sweet, true little voice, and you would try to sing along with her. You had a hard time keeping in tune, but you certainly tried and you never gave up. When we did personal appearances at rodeos and state fairs, Dodie did the singing—and you did the public speaking, and you had it all over Dodie in that department. You spoke with the aplomb of a Philadelphia lawyer. But you conquered singing, too. After you started singing in Kathy Johnston's Children's Choir at the Church in the Canyon you actually learned to sing a whole verse in perfect pitch. No one ever tried harder to sing well, unless it was your sister Cheryl who taught herself the same way. You had "stickability" in everything you did.

Do you remember when we all went to the Ohio State Fair at Columbus? At that time our television series had been on for quite a while, and it had a very high rating. A huge crowd came out to meet us at the airport. There wasn't adequate police protection, and as our plane landed people came running from every direction, pushing and shouting and waving in excitement. (Daddy was back in his home state!) You were on my lap as we hit the ground, and when you looked out of the window and saw all that commotion, with the police trying to control the crowd, you went into hysterics. It took a lot of explaining and assurance that these people loved us and didn't mean us any harm, that this wasn't fighting, or an air raid. You cried and buried your face in Pearl Wright's shoulder all the way into town. How sad it is that little children are frightened at such a tender age with man's inhumanity to man in war!

You and Dodie had such a good time playing in the hotel suite between shows, and you looked so sweet in your little costumes on the stage. You wore a spangled cowgirl costume, and Dodie wore a fancy Indian dress. Our musical director wrote a little Oriental band introduction for you, and an Indian one for Dodie. You two looked almost like twins at that age. How you enjoyed the Fair, and the big stuffed Teddy bears. What dreams I had for both of you! In my heart I dedicated both of you to the Lord, and prayed that He would show me what to do and lead you to accept Him and His will for your lives. One of my dearest memories of you is the way you looked the day you were baptized at the Chatsworth Methodist Church. You were still quite small. I can still see you and Dodie coming out of the junior church service with your hands full of flowers and carrying the jar of honey given you by the dear saint who led the junior church activities, Harold Johnson. Then there was the time when Rev. Mr. and Mrs. Doss, of the Methodist Church (In Redlands, California), brought their "international family" to join *our* international family at one of those pot-luck suppers in Whiteoak Hall at their church. I remember my pleasure and gratitude at seeing all you children, from such different lands and backgrounds, so happy and carefree together in God's house. Heaven must be like that.

There were the usual problems of adjustment for both you and Dodie. You had the edge on her when it came to adjustment, for you had been raised in an orphanage, where you had learned not to expect too much attention. Dodie had been the baby in the Rogers household since she was seven months old, with older brothers and sisters—and I'm afraid I had been too close to her after losing Robin. All of a sudden Dodie had to share—indeed, to give up more than half the attention she was accustomed to getting. You were new, from a foreign land, lovable, and needing help in many areas so you could take your place in our family. This is normal when a new baby arrives and the little sister or brother is still a baby, too! We had our moments, didn't we? Some of the moments were funny, and some not so funny—but with God's love and direction, and given understanding, we closed ranks and became a family.

When you came you were a head shorter than Dodie. She used to boss you around. You took it gracefully, on the whole, and didn't complain very much. We used to have a "hand-me-down" custom with the clothes, as most families do. When you were quite small you wore some of Dodie's clothes which she had outgrown, but which were still in good shape. Sandy wore Dusty's, the same way. But when new things were purchased for the older children, the smaller ones got something new, too. When you grew taller than Dodie, the shoe was on the other foot; she was given *your* hand-me-downs. To make things worse, you were beginning to get the upper hand in the "bossing around," for you were larger and stronger, Dodie complained about the hand-me-downs, and I said, "Honey, do you remember when Debbie wore yours? Turnabout is fair play, now isn't it?"

Then, just before the bus trip, Dodie came into the kitchen and asked me, "Mama, what does 'dominate' mean? Debbie says that when she gets to junior high with me, she is going to dominate me." Oh, the human equation! You girls had your moments, as all sisters do, but you had wonderful times, too, sharing secrets, hopes, dreams, fears, your likes and dislikes. Several days after you left us Dodie said, "Mom, when we were little, I used to cry when you were leaving on a trip with Daddy, and Debbie would try to make me forget it; when I was frightened or cold, she would get in my bed with me, or I with her." She said she would never forget the last swim you had together this summer, all by yourselves, in the pool at the house. You had so much fun figuring out new water stunts. You were like two little seals playing in the water.

I can remember these things, too, Debbie. I want to remember them; I want to write down *everything* I can recall about your time with us, so I can carry it in my heart until we meet again on that Beautiful Shore. God has created our minds so that we can retain just so much in the memory, but how wonderfully kind of Him to give us hearts in which we can hold the blessings of forgetfulness in the areas of grief and pain. At first, grief comes sweeping over us in thirty-foot waves. Gradually the waves become smaller; and if we trust in His wisdom and goodness and mercy, after a while understanding and acceptance and even joy start to roll in—slowly at first, in small waves, then, as time goes on, larger waves of peace and gratitude come. Through all our sorrow, if we know Christ as Saviour, deep within our souls there is peace, even when the tempest of shock, grief, and loss seems overwhelming.

I get great comfort in the words of Isaiah (61:1-3) in the Bible we used to read together:

> The Spirit of the Lord God is upon me; because the Lord hath anointed me to preach good tidings unto the meek; he hath

sent me to bind up the broken-hearted, to proclaim liberty to the captives, and the opening of the prison to them that are bound; To proclaim the acceptable year of the Lord, and the day of vengeance of our God; *to comfort all that mourn;* To appoint unto them that mourn in Zion, to give unto them beauty for ashes, the oil of joy for mourning, the garment of praise for the spirit of heaviness; that they might be called trees of righteousness, the planting of the Lord, that he might be glorified.

It is good, Debbie; while we mourn, you have been glorified—and I love and praise God for that.

I have been told that you are the first Korean orphan brought to this country by World Vision to pass from this world to heaven. I doubt that few, if any, Korean orphans have been as well known or publicized. I have also been told that the need of orphans all over the world is deepening into a real crisis. Somehow, I feel that your going is a sacrifice for all the others. You were always so unselfish, so ready to give your place to someone else. Perhaps God chose you to come to Him so that the attention of many people could be drawn to others like you abroad, and even here in America. Since you have been beckoned Home, God has led me to tell others, in this letter, about the blessings of housing an orphan—and there are so *many* blessings!

There was rich blessing for us when you and Dodie gave your hearts to Christ during the Billy Graham Crusade in Los Angeles in the summer of 1963. And I am so grateful for the good times we all had together on our trips—the trips to the state fairs, to rodeos in Canada, and to the Seattle World's Fair, to Banff and Lake Louise, to the thrilling Calgary Stampede. We were a happy family on the road. Do you remember the three-week camping trip we took to Jackson Hole, Wyoming, where we floated down the Snake River in a rubber tube? And Yellowstone, where Dodie was hospitalized, but where you, Daddy, and the boys caught so many trout in the big lake? And the happy days fishing near our cabin at Big Bear Lake? We had fun, didn't we? It was good—*so* good.

Every once in a while I have a twinge of regret as I think back to those days. I'm sorry now about fussing and scolding when you "snitched" the cucumbers, green peppers, and celery whenever I made a salad. I used to think you were part rabbit! How thrilled and proud you were when you learned to make my favorite lemon and garlic dressing all by yourself. I regret "harping," as so many mothers do, about leaving dirty dishes and orange peelings and apple cores and peanut shells in the kitchen or in front of the TV set in the living room. I wish I had not "gone into orbit" when you raided my clothes and my toilet articles. Such trivial things to get upset about—like refusing to let you sit on the washbowl and watch me "put on my face" and fix my hair when I was in such an all-fired hurry to meet a deadline somewhere. I suppose every mother wishes she could redo or undo many things when a beloved child leaves her. But honey, mothers aren't perfect, and children aren't, either. No one on this earth has ever been perfect, except our Lord Jesus Christ.

I'm still glad that I tried to be a good mother to you. Maybe I tried too hard, sometimes, but I loved you very much, and I told you so even when I corrected you. You would stiffen your little back, tighten your lips, not say much when you were reprimanded, and then you would stalk away. Yet, even when you were very small and had to be corrected, if I lost my temper and raised my voice you forgave so easily, and said you were sorry, too. And when I got back to a normal tone of voice and was a little ashamed and apologized for being cross, you would cry and hold out your little arms to me. During the last few years you would still clamp your lips in that tight line, toss your head, and stalk off stiff-legged to your room when correction was necessary, but when I would follow you into your room and try to explain the "why" of the correction, your eyes would start to twinkle and in a few minutes you would burst out laughing. What a spirit! What a girl!

How kind you were to all living creatures! I can still see the compassion in your eyes when you brought home the little sparrow you had found at the side of the road on your way home from school. You found an old birdcage in the laundry room; you put him in it so tenderly, and brought him water and tried to feed him. Amazingly, he "snapped out of it" in a few hours. I persuaded you to take him up the side of the mountain behind our house, away from the dogs, and give him his freedom. You saw the sense in that. Your heart was right, child—with God and all His creation.

How *inquisitive* you were! There was the day you were supposed to be taking a nap, when you were about four years old. I heard a shriek of terror. When I reached your room you were sitting on the floor, screaming in pain; you had pushed a bobby pin into the wall socket, and you got "the shock of your life." My heart sank when I saw your burned fingers, but the doctor took care of them, and after that you had a very healthy respect for wall plugs. I reminded myself then, as I have reminded myself in the last few days, that not a sparrow falls to the ground without the Father's knowledge, and that He allows us some pretty painful experiences because He has a *purpose* in allowing it.

We call some people "accident-prone," and I suppose the description might fit you, but I would say that you were not so much accident-prone as oblivious to the presence of danger. During the recent Beatle bedlam, I was concerned about you girls placing your radio so close to the tub while you were taking your baths; knowing how you jumped around all over the place, I was afraid you might knock the radio into the water. Countless were the times that I cautioned you about darting out into the street in front of cars—laughing, talking, blithely assuming that nothing could or would harm you. There were times when you would take off after dark on your bikes, to ride down past the barns to the gate for the evening paper, or when you walked over to a friend's house in the gathering darkness, promising to be back in half an hour. When an hour was past and you still were not home, I would rush to the phone—and you would breeze into the kitchen, amazed that I should be so worried. You had no fear of the night. That helped me so much on the dark night of August 17, when you "crossed the Jordan"—I know it was without fear, that the night held no terror for you, that underneath you were the Everlasting Arms. There never had to be a light burning in your room, even when you were a wee one.

But to get back to your birthday, on August 14. After we left Marion's that afternoon, we celebrated first by going to see Daddy at the hospital, and then to dinner at the Italian pizza place,

Solino's, where you ate enough for six grownups. For some reason, neither Dodie nor I felt like eating that day. Then we went to a store and bought some new stretch jeans and patchwork print tops for you and Dodie to wear playing miniature golf that night, and then to Pacific Ocean Park the next day, where our friend Carlie was helping you celebrate your birthday.

For no apparent reason, I felt ill all day Friday, and I just couldn't play golf that night; I waited in the car while you and Dodie played. I had strange misgivings about your trip to Pacific Ocean Park the next day; I was unaccountably afraid that you girls might get hurt on the roller coaster, and I worried about the traffic, and the sharp mountain curves in the road. I was just plain uneasy. Was it premonition, or what? Who knows? When Carlie came for you on Saturday morning, I asked her to put up the top of her convertible, and drive slowly, and be careful of her precious cargo. I spent several hours with Daddy at the hospital, got home about 3:30, and started getting dinner ready. When you didn't arrive at the promised hour of four, I really began to worry. You showed up at 5:15, tired out and happy, and I was both relieved and chagrined at my needless worry. I should have known that God was holding you in the hollow of His hand.

The next day was Sunday. How pretty you looked in your green skirt and striped blouse! You had rolled your hair for a nice, soft "bubble" look the night before, and you came waltzing into my room and stood before the mirror and asked me, "How do I look?" I replied, "You look lovely— pretty." You arched your thick brows and stated, "If you ask me, I think I'm beautiful!"

We laughed, and I reminded you of what Grandma Smith told me when I was a child: "Pretty is as pretty does." You said, "Oh, yes, Mommy. I remember. We must first be pretty *inside*." You were pretty inside as well as outside. As a matter of fact, I was beginning to be a little uneasy over your maturing so fast. I wanted you to take your time. The big boys, as well as the little ones, were beginning to "notice" you. I grew up too fast, and I didn't want you to do that. In temperament, you, Cheryl, and I were very much alike in childhood. I was inquisitive, always on the go, loving attention and getting it—very much an extrovert. Extroverts "have a blast," to quote one of your favorite expressions, but they overdo it sometimes, to their own hurt. I know, because I was like that. Honey, if I tried to hold you down occasionally it wasn't because I wanted to be "possessive" but (I wouldn't admit this even to myself) because I feared your high spirit. Bless your heart, you took it so well. Yours was a sweet spirit. I still feel it here in this house—especially in your room, and in your favorite "hangout," the kitchen.

You and Dodie complemented each other beautifully. You were an extrovert, she an introvert. You had many friends and many more acquaintances; Dodie's friends haven't been so numerous, but they have been close. When you left, Dodie was able to reach out in friendship to a greater extent because, I am sure, she missed you so much, and she was trying to compensate for her loss. You loved dolls, pretty clothes, girl chit-chat, experimenting in the kitchen, and having your friends over or visiting them. Dodie loves books, records, her school work, talking with her friends on the phone, reading comics—and romping and roaming with the dogs on the ranch. You were boisterous, Dodie quiet. Since you left, the house has been so quiet. One thing you both had in common—your love of God and the church. Since you went away I have seen Dodie kneel at the altar and pray at the close of the sermon. I am sure her spiritual communion with you is still warm in her heart.

Your room has become our family chapel. We have moved your bed out of the room and we put an altar in its place, next to the big window. Some folks in the Methodist Church in Chatsworth, knowing your love of flowers, sent a beautiful rose bush, a lovely hisbiscus plant, and some beautiful pink azalea plants. Speaking of azaleas, they came to America by way of Korea. I shall always see your pretty little face in every pink azalea. We have planted these gifts under the big window in the chapel. Early each morning, I go in and pray and read the Bible, and just sit there in quiet communion with you and God. I remember in those moments that Jesus said, "Lo, I am with you always," and that Paul said, "To be absent from the body is to be present with the Lord." Kneeling there, it seems to me that the Lord and you are standing at my shoulder. It has a great healing power. My Bible says, "In quietness and confidence shall be your strength."

You and Dodie shared your birthday gifts; before we left for Sunday school at the Chapel in the Canyon that morning, you promised Dodie that she could wear your things after you had worn them. I got a real thrill that morning, watching you in the Youth Choir processional. You were so pleased to be singing in the "big" choir. I sat in the front row with Kathy Johnston, and across the aisle sat Dodie with Joanne Russell and her little brother David. As Larry was preaching, you suddenly tried to "wig-wag" a message to me about Dodie. I frowned at you and shook my head, because I didn't want anyone to be distracted from listening to an excellent sermon. You kept it up, and finally I turned to look at Dodie, who was quite pale, her lips saying silently, "Mama, I'm sick." Kathy Johnston quickly took her out, and over to the manse.

We got her home and put her to bed, gave her some soda pop for her upset tummy, and fixed lunch for you and the boys. After lunch, when Dodie was still having her troubles, I asked you not to go to the Mexican Orphanage in Tia Juana the next day with the other youngsters from the church. I wanted you to wait until Dodie and I could go with you—perhaps on the next trip, after Daddy was home from the hospital. You said, "Mama, *please*—I have been planning on it, and Joanne and Kathy Russell are counting on me. This was to be part of my birthday celebration. Please,

please—it isn't fair to keep me home because Dodie can't go!" You had me there. Since this was your birthday, and since so many adults were going along in the bus to Tia Juana, and since it was an errand of love for orphaned children, I gave in, thinking it would be an added rich spiritual blessing for you. And it was. It proved to be your most important journey—into the light of God's presence.

The Russells called for you around 5 P.M. You were so excited that I had to call you back from their car to kiss me goodbye. You called out kiddingly to Dodie, "Bye! I'll try not to have too good a time, Dodie!" You three girls were deposited at the home of the Whites, where you were to spend the night in sleeping bags on the living-room floor. You were to leave early Monday morning on the drive to Tia Juana, stop in the town for lunch and a little quick shopping, visit the orphans with your gifts of clothes and food and toys, and stop at Knott's Berry Farm on the way home. Larry (Rev. Larry White, of the Church in the Canyon) told me that you girls had a great "giggling spree" that night in the living room, and that he had to come in twice to "settle you down." He was driving the bus the next day, and he needed *some* rest!

You had the time of your life, and I'm so glad for that. Mrs. Pigot, who was in charge of the "team" you were on, told us how delighted you were to see and hold the children in the orphanage. How I wish I had a film of that, to look at when my heart needs a lift! You and several of your friends had your pictures taken in Tia Juana by one of those wandering street photographers; you were wearing a big Mexican sombrero and serape, and with your deep Hawaiian tan you really looked like a part of old Mexico. I have pasted that picture in your scrapbook—which you entitled "All About Me!"

I hadn't the slightest misgiving about your going on that bus trip, Debbie. All that day—Monday, the 17th—I wasn't feeling quite up to par, physically, but I did the household chores; "Granny" Miner (Mrs. Ruth Miner) came at noon to stay with Dodie and Sandy while I went to see Daddy at the convalescent home. It was there, for the first time, that I began to feel strangely disquieted within myself. As I was driving home around 4:30, I felt so disturbed that I started to pray for God's help. I began by thanking Him for His love and long-suffering patience with me, asking Him to help me now to "lose myself" completely in Him, and to do His will through me, and to put my restless, disturbed heart and mind at rest—in "perfect peace," in faith. I needed to relax in Him. I knew there were areas in my thinking that needed to be taken over by His Holy Spirit. It was like Jacob wrestling with the angel; I didn't want to "let go" of God until He had blessed me with His peace. He did just that. By the time I turned the car into the driveway at the ranch, His peace was upon me.

I needed that peace badly—for now came the shattering blow.

I remember what a strange afternoon it was—warm, restless, with turbulent winds. As I walked toward the kitchen door, I saw Granny watching me, with a strange expression on her face, through the kitchen window. I didn't hear the motor of the refrigerating unit as I stepped into the house, and I called out, "Ruth, it's hot; isn't the cooler working?" Ruth looked at me steadily for a moment, took me by the arm and said quietly but so desperately, "Look, Dale—there's been an accident—the church bus—coming home from Tia Juana—Debbie and Joanne Russell are gone—with the Lord."

Just like that. I couldn't grasp it for a long moment, and then, from the deep recesses of my soul, I resisted: "No! No! No!" Then, "Please, Jesus, help me! My baby again!" I cried out for the grace to accept it.

On August 24, just twelve years ago, the Lord had lifted little Robin from my grasp. Here, all over again, was the same rending, tearing anguish, only sharper this time, for Robin had been ill all through her short little life, but you had been so vital, so alive. At that moment Dusty—bless him!—came to me, grasped me by the shoulders, and pleaded, "Mom, Debbie is with the Lord; you know that. Listen, Mom: you have always depended on Him and trusted Him. You'll have to trust Him now!" I needed that. I told him that I was so grateful that Debbie was ready to meet her Lord. And I needed Sandy, who came to me so overwhelmed that he couldn't speak: he just put his hand on my shoulder, and there was something in his touch that words couldn't say.

Then I couldn't find Dodie, and the panic came again. Granny had told her the awful news before I reached home, and she had run out in tears to the refuge of the rocks behind the house, with the dogs all around her. Jack Brooks, our gardener, and his wife Sylvia came in to comfort. What would I have done without them?

It's strange, honey, but about the time of the collision, Granny was ironing in the kitchen, and your red bicycle, just outside the window, fell to the pavement with a clatter. She couldn't understand it, for your bike was stationary in the bike stand. About two weeks earlier there was the persistent wailing of our dog Bullet in the night. I heard it, uneasily, remembering how Robin's dog Lana had also cried so in the night before her going away. I woke Daddy to listen, and he said, "Oh, he's probably heard an ambulance siren, and it hurts his ears." Do dogs *know*?

A thousand and one confusions pressed on me now. The telephone was ringing incessantly, family friends were arriving, the newspapers wanted details—and there was my deepening concern for Daddy in the hospital. He had a small TV set in his room; I called his nurse and asked her to take it away until he could be told about the accident, for I knew that radio and TV would carry it immediately. His surgeon told him, and then I talked with him on the phone. This hit us so hard—both of us! I was afraid to go to you at the scene of the crash, because of what might happen to Daddy. I'm glad now I didn't go; I could have done nothing there, and my family needed me so much.

Dodie said, "Mom, why can't I go to heaven, too, and be with Debbie? There are such awful things happening in the world!" Dodie would say that; she was always so worried about losing her little sister when you were both small. Every time you were hurt — when you would fall off your bike, or trip over your own feet—Dodie would be frantic with fear. Do you remember the day in Daddy's den when you fell and hit your head on a sharp corner of the table, opening that deep gash half an inch from your left eye? Dodie screamed, "Is she going to die?" Or the day you had the high fever, and I rocked you in my lap in the Boston rocker for four hours? Dodie stood beside us all through it, tears in her eyes, afraid you would die. Was that prophetic?

But now Dodie looked beyond you to all the sadness in the world, to the sadness and sorrow of so many others who were suffering just as we were suffering. She was thinking what so many of us say—"What's the *use?* How can we have any confidence in anything or anybody, when such things happen?" Yet when we know God, we have every reason to be confident, for then we live in a house not built with human hands, but eternal, in the heavens—a "house" that will not be dissolved by any accident, or tragedy, or murder, or even atomic blast. Our spiritual house will remain intact! I said to poor Dodie, "We must trust in the Lord with all our hearts, and lean not on our own understanding." When He is ready, He will beckon.

I feel somehow that He was beckoning you and Joanne that afternoon on the bus, for you kept coming up to the front, wanting to stand near Larry, who was driving, and talking with him. How many times I let my beloved Tom, Dusty, and Dodie, when they were toddlers, stand up in the car and hold on to the dashboard, or stand up on the front seat with nothing to hold to but my neck—no seat belts! Now that I am older and have seen so many highway accidents, I know better. A bus is larger and sturdier than a car. Even commercial buses allow people to stand where there aren't enough seats, or when they are preparing to get off. The last thing I said to you on Sunday afternoon was, "Have a wonderful time, honey, and obey Larry and Ernestine." Larry told you and Joanne twice to go back to your seats. But I know, darling, how you could "wheedle" people around your little finger when you wanted something. You and Joanne got into an argument with some boys who had been standing up front, and you said it was your turn now—you could see so much more up there! Larry loved you, and so you went up to the front, and there you were when the front left tire blew. I have had a few blowouts myself, and I know what a struggle I had holding an ordinary car on the road. When this tire blew, the weight of the bus with sixty-six passengers sent the steering wheel into an uncontrollable spin. Dusty told me that they were three days at the hospital trying to get the varnish from that wheel out of Larry's hands; he gripped the wheel so hard, but it was too much for any man. The bus swerved into the oncoming traffic and the impact of the station wagon that struck the bus was powerful, quick, and incisive. God was merciful to me in not letting me be there to see it. I only know that your going was quick. Perhaps the "powers that be"—the political powers—in California will realize now the urgent need to widen that twenty-one-mile stretch of super dangerous highway with its four lanes and no barrier between. Attendants at the hospital in Oceanside are bitter at the needless fatal accidents occurring on what they call "Slaughter Alley"—an unbelievably high number in the past two years.

Yet, notwithstanding all this, I know that God was on His throne as it happened, and that His heart broke, as ours broke. I cannot say He caused it, for God is not the author of confusion, or sin, or sickness, or death. But He knew that this bus carried those who believed in Him and who put their trust in Him—and that heaven is infinitely sweeter than earth. I believe it was allowed for His high purpose. A letter from a dear lady who followed the bus in and out of Tia Juana that day said it was a wonderful blessing to her to hear the children and the grownups in the bus singing hymns in praise of God. Our God is good. He prepared you well, for your greatest adventure.

How wonderful to go to heaven in a church bus! That is far better, so much better, than going in a "hot rod" accident, or in one caused by a drinking driver. I have been told that a policeman, arriving on the scene of the wreck that afternoon, dropped to his knees and asked God to take him back into His fold. This man had strayed in strange pastures—and now, because of what he saw on that road, he had come back. As Larry said in his first sermon two weeks after the accident: "The real tragedy of this accident would be if no lives were changed toward Christ." I agree. The Bible says that our lives are but a vapor. It is eternity that counts. Where will we spend *eternity?* God has the answer to that question in His Word: "Believe on the Lord Jesus Christ, and thou shalt be saved . . . " (Acts 16:31). This is why I sorrow with hope, for you believed on Him and you loved Him. Just a week before the accident I saw you kneel at the church altar and give yourself to Him in rededication after the service. Paul says, in Galatians 2:20, "I am crucified with Christ: nevertheless I live; yet not I, but Christ liveth in me: and the life which I now live in the flesh I live by the faith of the Son of God, who loved me, and gave himself for me." Except Christ be in me, Debbie, my way would indeed be impossibly long and dreary.

We must personally get smaller and He must get larger in our lives. John the Baptist said of

Jesus, "He must increase, but I must decrease" (John 3.30). My darling, your decrease has already increased the number in His fold in a miraculous way. Letters telling me about that are pouring in (we shall read a few of them later in this book).

Our doctor gave me a sedative to help me sleep that night, since I had to make all the arrangements; Daddy was away, and the Russells were at Oceanside with their daughter Kathy, who was in serious condition. The little coats that had clothed the bright spirits of you and Joanne had been taken by the coroner to San Diego. Mr. Russell and their family physician went to identify them. I talked with the coroner, who suggested that I call Forest Lawn in Los Angeles, where you might be prepared for your memorial service.

When little Robin left us, Daddy did all these things for me. Now I had to do it. Judy Whisenant drove me out next day to see Daddy, and then to Forest Lawn. I took along your sixth-grade graduation dress; Granny and I had decided you should wear it. How sweet you looked on that graduation day— and how hard I shopped to find just the right dress, little knowing that you would wear it for your Big Commencement. You loved pink, and so did Joanne, so pink was chosen.

The Lord was very present with me all through this; He gave me strength and peace to do what had to be done. The night of the accident, after much prayer, Dodie, Judy, and I slept together in the master bedroom. About 3:30 A.M. I was awakened by the sound of anguished crying; I got up and went into Granny's room, thinking it was she—but no, she thought it was I! Then, as I went to the living room, Bowser, our dog, was crying like a human being. I knelt at the altar and prayed for spiritual strengthening while he cried. He loved you, Debbie. Who didn't? Then I went to the big Bible, and my eyes fell on the twelfth chapter of Hebrews:

Wherefore seeing we also are compassed about with so great a cloud of witnesses, let us lay aside ever weight, and the sin which doth so easily beset us, and let us run with patience the race that is set before us, looking unto Jesus the author and finisher of our faith; who for the joy that was set before him endured the cross, despising the shame, and is set down at the right hand of the throne of God. For consider him that endured such contradiction of sinners against himself, lest ye be wearied and faint in your minds. Ye have not resisted unto blood, striving against sin. And ye have forgotten the exhortation which speaketh unto you as unto children, My son, despise not thou the chastening of the Lord, nor faint when thou art rebuked of him: For whom the Lord loveth he chasteneth, and scourgeth every son whom he receiveth. If ye endure chastening, God dealeth with you as with sons; for what son is he whom the father chasteneth not?

Then further on:

Now no chastening for the present seemeth to be joyous, but grievous: nevertheless afterward it yieldeth the peaceful fruit of righteousness unto them which are exercised thereby. Wherefore lift up the hands which hang down, and the feeble knees; And make straight paths for your feet, lest that which is lame be turned out of the way; but let it rather be healed.

I had my answer; I went back to bed, and slept soundly for three hours. God does answer prayer. He has answered mine, every time. Sometimes the answer is "Yes." Sometimes it is "No." But He always answers. *The secret is to expect it.*

Reverend Ralph Hoopes, the minister of Valley Presbyterian Church and a long-time friend, came out with David Whisenant, Judy's husband, and we had wonderful prayer together, along with other close friends. Ralph accepted my request that he speak at the service; Ernestine White said she wanted to take part on behalf of the Chapel, since Debbie and Joanne had been her pupils.

Larry was still hospitalized at Oceanside. Reverend Leonard Eilers, an old friend and chaplain of our Hollywood Christian Group, would offer the prayer. Grandma Smith came (from Texas), and Cheryl, Marion, Linda, Art and Mary Jo Rush, Pat O'Shea, Majorie Hamilton, Kathy Johnston, and Carlie. Friends from Chatsworth brought flowers, and food, and tears of love—telegrams and cables and letters poured in from all over the United States and even from abroad. We were so grateful. Tom and Barbara and their children were somewhere in Arizona in their camp in the mountains. We were never able to contact them because their radio wasn't working. They didn't know you were gone until after the services were over. Granny Miner, whom you loved so dearly and who loved you the same, was with me, steady as the Rock of Gibraltar.

The coroner thought it best to keep your caskets closed, and we all agreed. But my heart ached to see you just once more. The day before the funeral, Grandma Smith, Art, Judy, the Russels and I met at Forest Lawn, just to go into the slumber room and spend a few minutes beside the caskets. The man in charge called Art aside and said we might view your "vacated houses" after all, for a minute, and my heart was soothed. Somehow, since I had lacked the courage to look at little Robin's body, and was troubled later about it, I just had to touch your pretty hands and smooth the rich, dark hair once more. It had hurt me that I wasn't with you when you departed, and

I felt compelled to do this. Was this selfish desire? Maybe so, but I felt that the Lord approved, that He was urging me, and it proved such a blessing. I prayed silently as we went up in the elevator. You and Joanne were in a double room, with an archway between. As I went in, there was no fear, only love—Christ had cushioned me for this, darling.

How sweet you looked! You seemed about sixteen years old instead of twelve! So ladylike, poised, and peaceful—your hair was beautiful, complete with bangs, bubble, and white bow in front. You had a half-smile—almost a Mona Lisa. Under your graceful fingers was the little blue plush dog you had bought at Pacific Ocean Park on Saturday. I knelt there and thanked the Lord for the nine years He had loaned you to us. I asked Him to forgive me for any failures in mothering you, and for any possessiveness I might have shown with you and any of the children. I told Him that I realized now that none of my loved ones had ever belonged completely to me; they belonged to Him, and now I was giving you back to Him with gratitude, and henceforth I would place all of the children in His hands. I prayed Him to direct my efforts to serve those I loved, in the future. Then all of us stood and prayed together the Lord's Prayer.

I felt a holy warmth and joy fill my entire being, transcending all thoughts of mortality. I was with you and Joanne in eternity. What lay before me in that slumber room was merely your earthly cloak, to be tenderly laid aside, for now you were clothed in the radiance of the Spirit. My heart took wings; I went to the side of Joanne's mother and said to her, "Jean, we must not weep. We must rejoice! Our girls have graduated. Let's give them a wonderful Commencement Service."

The next morning our family decided that we would dress for the service just as we had dressed for your sixth-grade commencement. Dodie wore white, I wore a pink dress with black accessories, and a short veil to screen the tear furrows of the last two days. The boys wore their "Sunday suits." Before the Forest Lawn limousine arrived, I knelt at our altar and asked God to give me strength that I might be a good Christian witness at the service. With all my heart I wanted the world to know that He is the answer and strength of my life. Then I went outside and picked three of the prettiest rosebuds I could find for you. He heard my prayer, for as we entered the Church of the Recessional at Forest Lawn, filled with beautiful floral displays for you and Joanne, I called the attendant and asked if he would place a new gold cross around your neck, since the one you usually wore had been lost in the wreck. As he adjusted the chain, I placed the rosebuds in your lovely hands. Somehow I knew that you and Joanne were aware of the wonderful tributes being paid you. I could almost hear you say, "Hey, Mom! What a blast! Is this all for *me*?" One week after the funeral I received a letter that said, "Dear Dale: When I heard about the bus accident it was bad enough. When I heard that the daughter of Dale and Roy Rogers was in it, I wondered if your strength would hold. You had been through so much. I saw you on television at the funeral and I think your face told the story. It was a terrible agony for you, but there was a peace on your face that is seldom seen these days." Praise the Lord!

The service was beautiful. Ralph Hoopes gave a blessed message of Christian hope, and closed with this poem:

"I'll lend you for a little time,
    a child of Mine," He said,
"For you to love the while she lives,
    and mourn when she is dead.
It may be six or seven years,
    or twenty-two or three,
But will you, till I call her back,
    take care of her for Me?
She'll bring her charms to gladden you,
    and tho' her stay be brief,
You will have lovely memories
    as solace for your grief.

"I cannot promise she will stay,
    since all from earth return,
But there are lessons taught down here
    I want this child to learn.
I have looked the world-wide over
    in my search for teachers true,
And from the throngs that crowd life's lanes,
    I have selected you.

Now will you give her all your love,
    nor think the labor vain,
Nor hate Me when I come to call
    to take her back again?"

We fancied that we heard them say,
    "Dear Lord, Thy will be done!
For all the joy Thy child will bring,
    the risk of grief we run.
We will shelter her with tenderness,
    we will love her while we may,
And for the happiness we have now,
    forever grateful stay.
But shall the angels call for her
    much sooner than we planned,
We shall brave the bitter grief that comes
    and try to understand."

Mrs. White spoke lovingly of you and Joanne as her Sunday school pupils and singers in the Junior Choir. She reminded us that while you had enjoyed so much singing in the Chapel Choir, you were enjoying even more singing in the celestial one. Reverend Eilers and Dr. Hayward prayed, and then, as we walked back into the mausoleum for the final committal, I was conscious of an unearthly peace in my heart. My eyes fell on the marble open book on the threshold, and I read the words graven there:

On that golden slumber, the worn spirit is shed for the blazing mantle of immortality
                      —HUDSON.

My heart sang as I drank in the meaning of those words: "Debbie has her wings! She is free!"

You said this spring that there were two places you wanted to see—Hawaii and Switzerland. Well, you saw Hawaii this summer, and somehow I feel that God has granted your second wish and shown you Switzerland, for with your quick and questing spirit you would be everywhere at once! A fine Christian minister said to me once that he believes our departed ones "are in the bleachers of a huge arena — watching us who are still here on earth. We are players, the contestants. They know the game of life and they are rooting for us as we struggle." He believes they are very close to us, but operating "on a different wave length." Then, of course, there is that Scripture in Hebrews 12 which says that we are surrounded by a great cloud of witnesses. That could also mean that as Christians we are surrounded by nonbelievers who are watching us to see if Christ is really what we claim He is in our lives—watching the Christians walk, sometimes on a tightrope, as I am walking now.

As we left Forest Lawn I said to Judy, "There is no despair in my heart, only joy for Debbie"—and I meant it. Joy that you will never be cut by disillusionment, never know the pangs of bereavement, or the anguish of guilt that comes to all of us through willfully sinning against God's law. Yes, my child, you are truly and forevermore blest.

You should see the thousands of letters that have been sent to comfort us! It will take weeks for me to read them all, but I want to tell you about a few I have read and loved, up to now. A lady from Florida says in her letter, "The darker the night, the tighter the grip on the Master's hand!" That says volumes, doesn't it? Another lady sent a poem about the sailing of a ship: when a ship leaves port, those standing on the shore say sadly, "There she goes!" But those on the Other Shore cry gladly, "Here she *comes!*" I love that—and I love to think of all those who were waiting to welcome you on the Other Shore—they were a greater number than those who saw you go!

Do you remember Lolly Deats, our friend over in Pacific Palisades? She wrote this: "I can barely imagine how such a loss might be, and yet, hearing my twelve-year-old pray for your Dodie almost shames me. Their faith is so very simple and so secure, and yet she has prayed for Dodie that 'she may not worry if they ever had any arguments or if Debbie is lonely, because she's fine.' My daughter seemed to understand so quickly how Dodie must feel, and it has made her more conscious of her feelings toward her own sisters and toward her awareness of heaven as an actuality. . . . I sometimes think that this basic certainty of our future life can almost shape our present atitude. It seems to give an added power and confidence to the smallest things. Beneath your loss and grief is the inexpressible gratitude that you had placed Debbie in God's hands in time. . . . There is true release, true rest, in knowing that we have done what we were given to do. . . . It always surprises people somehow to see sorrow hit a Christian, as though we should be immune to it in this world. And when they see us weep as they weep, ache as they ache—and yet with the hope and assurance gradually coming through to hold us together, the knowledge that our loved one have been placed in God's hands, they can't help but wonder if perhaps they, too, shouldn't seek Him before it is too late. It's hard, and sometimes it seems unfair, that God can use our sorrow as a prod to others, but I guess it is for this that He strengthens us. . . . I don't know. . . . Yes, I *do* know that it's never easy and only a fool would welcome it, but this one thing He has promised: it will never be more than we can bear, even though at the time we may think so. . . ."

A friend in Encinitas, California, wrote telling me of something her daughter-in-law had said: "Mom, I think God has something important for that little girl to do. How much He must have loved her, to take her so young! Maybe He took her because if she had lived through the crash, she would have been in pain, or lived out her life in a hospital. Life is a wonderful gift. We make the best of it by living out each day to the fullest. But when the Savior calls, 'Follow Me,' we should rise without a backward glance and answer, 'Lord, I'm coming.' Our Saviour was very busy after the wreck, as He always is. Picture in your mind His picking up those broken ones and taking them to the Father, comforting them, drying their tears, telling them not to be afraid, for they had things to do there. . . . Death is not the end of life; it is the beginning. . . ."

A second-grade Sunday school teacher tells me this: "When I asked the children if they wanted to pray for Deborah Lee and Joanne, they said they would rather pray for the mothers, fathers, sisters, and families . . . They explained to me that Debbie and Joanne were very happy with Jesus. . . . This has been a real blessing to the teachers' hearts. . . ."

And Lowell Ditzen, our friend and the director of the National Presbyterian Center in Washington, wrote: "As you know so deeply, the spirit of your sweet daughter not only adds light to the heavenly hosts but she goes on and on here, blessing us all. . . ."

These aren't just letters, Debbie dear; they are human Christian hearts reaching out toward you—and me.

Then there is Mrs. Taylor, in Canoga Park, who wrote this poem for us:

> Your daughter has this day
>   Joined His band above.
> Tho' born in strife she was led to you
>   To learn His faithful love.

Sorrow now has filled your hearts,
 Yet by His will you still abide.
Perfection still is in His plan;
We know He has not lied.

There are no two ways about it . . .,
 This earth — it can't compare
With the home He has in store for us,
 And for "Angels Unaware."

The mighty task He gave to you
 Must have been complete, today,
As on her merry mission
 He surely heard her pray.

Tho' her love has left consolation,
 There's still an empty chair.
Welcome it, Dear Lord,
 Let them see Your comfort there.

She was so young and innocent—
 Yet please try to understand—
Time is not measured by clocks,
 After we have touched His hand.
When Jesus died upon the Cross,
 He only asked our trust.
No small worries troubled Him,
 Such as if the nails would rust.

So when He takes a loved one
    We weep and ask Him, Why?
No questions should we have of Him,
    Of His majesty, Most High.

You know her crown was polished;
    He must have seen it shine.
He trusted you with that, but
    He put her next in line.

The tears may come with human thoughts;
    Your reward you've yet to see—
When heaven opens its doors to you,
    There's Debbie waiting, patiently.

I needed those letters so, to help me through the dark hours that kept coming, night and day. I dreamed one night that Daddy, Dodie, and I were in the living room of a new house. For some reason, I turned to look at the fireplace, and there you stood, combing your pretty dark hair, looking into the mirror over the mantle. I cried out, "Debbie, it's you!" You turned to look at me and smiled, just as you used to smile on Sunday morning coming out to the car. But your eyes! I walked closer and looked deep into them. They were different, wondrous. I seemed to lose myself in them. They were wise, compassionate—eternity was in them. I tore myself away to say, "Daddy, Dodie — it's Debbie, look!" They stared at me, and they said, "Mama, what's the matter with you? What are you talking about?" I looked back toward the mantle — you had disappeared. That dream is still vivid, and it has God's meaning in it.

Another night, I was reading my Bible about midnight, and I distinctly heard your squeaky bicycle out on the driveway — I had heard those scraping brakes many times while you were with us, and I was always saying we must oil them. When I heard that noise that night, I thought, "It can't be! Who on earth would be riding Debbie's bike this time of night? Maybe it's some teenage prowlers just goofing around the place." Then my mind said, "With God all things are possible. He has sent this sound to you to let you know that Debbie is alive, because He is the resurrection — and she is with and in Him."

Oh yes, my child, there have been those hours, hours of wonder and awe and sadness. I cannot say that I have not wept in sorrow. There was a popular song not so long ago called "Cry Me a River." Honey, I've cried a whole sea of tears. No matter how many children a mother may have — and goodness knows, I've had a "passel" of them — when one is taken there is left a void. No child can ever take another child's place in a mother's heart, for each child makes his own place. When a tree is uprooted it leaves a hole in the ground — but when transplanted, it beautifies the new site. So it is with you. You have been transplanted in a new and wondrous place, to go on growing in God's own garden. He had the right to pluck two lovely buds on August 17th. He had planted them on this earth, tended them, and He wanted to transplant them There. Who are we to say that He must wait until the bloom fades and withers, simply because we want to enjoy the blossoms longer?

It is as Lowell Ditzen wrote me: you go on and on *here,* in all the beauty of your blossoming youth. Your transplanting has caused some changes at the Double-R Bar ranch. The house is quieter, but there is more kindness now, more thoughtfulness all the way around. We've learned some valuable lessons. The other day I asked Daddy if he minded giving Dusty a very expensive sports coat he loved — he had only worn it three or four times, and it looked so nice on Dusty. Daddy smiled and said, "You can go through this house and take anything I have and do what you want with it; in the last few weeks, I have learned that material possessions mean nothing."

I too have learned some lessons. I have learned that nothing belongs to me — not Debbie, not all my other loved ones, not my material possessions. Even my own life belongs to God. He has merely let me enjoy them for a season. I pray that He will direct all my dealings with them, from now on. I have learned that "This is the day which the Lord hath made; we will rejoice and be glad in it" (Psalm 118:24). We cannot call back yesterday and we do not have tomorrow. Now is the accepted time of salvation. Moment by moment, I am kept in His love. Someone has aptly said, "The only things we can take with us when we leave this world are the things we have given away." And when we give ourselves away to the Lord, He saves our souls for all eternity.

I do not pretend to know the answer to why God called you and Joanne home so soon. I only know that I trust His wisdom, and that I love Him with all there is in me. "In Him I live and move and have my being." He sees the end from the beginning. If I trust and obey Him, He has promised that He will direct my path upward. God does not break us with testings; He means to make us stronger and more useful. He comforts us in the testing, so that we may comfort others, when they are tested, with "the comfort wherewith we ourselves are comforted..." (II Corinthians 1:4). I only know that I want to be used by Him, as He sees fit, in the earthly years that I have left. It isn't for me to ask "Why?" — but, "Lord, what would You have me do?"

Two weeks ago, at the Galilean Hour at our church, someone requested the little song, "Go, Tell It on the Mountain, That Jesus Christ Is Born." Kathy Johnston was sitting beside me; she choked up and said, "No, no; that was Debbie's song" — and Kathy couldn't sing it. Later I remembered the afternoon our family sang that song at one of the Easter Share-the-Blessings Brunches at the Beverly Hilton, sponsored by the Hollywood Christian Group. For some reason, you became shy all of a sudden, and refused to look out at the audience. I was playing the piano and you, Dodie, Dusty, Sandy, and Daddy were grouped around and we were singing a little arrangement of this song. You and Dodie sang the verses and the rest of us joined in on the chorus. Every time a new verse came up, you would turn away from the mike and turn your back on the audience, and I would reach out with my right hand and turn your face back where it belonged. It got quite a laugh — when I saw it on film I laughed, too, for I was such a typical "stage mamma." But as I think of it now, I don't laugh — the song means so much, in retrospect. You know, you came all the way from war-torn Korea to make your home in a free America where you learned about Jesus, loved Him, and gave over your life to Him. If we could hear you speak, I know you would be saying, "Yes, hurry! Go tell it on every mountain in the world that Jesus Christ is the answer. He is coming back again, and when He does, I'm coming with Him, along with all the others who accepted Him!"

You will never be a closed chapter in my book of life, Debbie; you will live in my heart and I shall go right on singing the Lord's praises until He calls me home, too, to sing in that Great Choir of the Heavenly Host. I am so glad that all in our family have accepted Christ, and God's guidance in life and in death. One day we shall have a great reunion. I'm looking forward to that. But until then — until then — until then, as Stuart Hamblen wrote in his wonderful song, "Until then, my heart will go on singing. . . ."

I read in the Book of the Prophet Jeremiah (33:3) in my Bible: "Call unto me, and I will answer thee, and shew thee great and mighty things, which thou knowest not." I will go on calling on Him, as I have for so long. He has, and He always will answer me. He has shown me mighty things, and some very hard things which I never expected — but always, when I trusted him, blessings followed in abundance. "For unto whomsoever much is given, of him shall much be required..." (Luke 12:48). He has given me much, and on August 17, 1964, He required a sweet sacrifice.

The Lord giveth, and the Lord taketh away; blessed be the name of the Lord.

And I know that in His infinite love, He will give again.

Lovingly,
Your Mother